Asperger Syndrome Explained

How to Understand and Communicate

When Someone You Love Has

Asperger's Syndrome

Sara Elliott Price

Published in The USA by:

Success Life Publishing

125 Thomas Burke Dr.

Hillsborough, NC 27278

Copyright © 2015 by Sara Elliott Price

2nd Edition

ISBN-10: 1511636432

Disclaimer

Table of Contents

Introduction

I want to thank you for downloading, *"Asperger Syndrome Explained: How to Understand and Communicate When Someone You Love Has Asperger's Syndrome."*

By deciding to download this book you have taken the first step to overcoming the difficulties you may be experiencing because of Asperger's Syndrome. Whether it's a friend, relative or even yourself who has Asperger's, this book gives you the understanding you need to have better communication with a person who has this disorder.

Asperger's Syndrome may be one of the most misunderstood disorders facing the world today. People with Asperger's are mistakenly judged by others as being unsympathetic, angry, careless and self-absorbed. Nothing could be further from the truth.

Asperger's Syndrome is not a disorder that affects intelligence but rather a disorder that affects the ability to communicate like those around them. People with Asperger's look at the world around them in a way that is completely different from most of us, which is why it is sometimes hard for us to understand them and know how to cope with this disorder.

The average "Aspie" will be very intelligent, have a high level of OCD (Obsessive Compulsive Disorder) and will lack in social skills. They don't easily pick up or understand normal social cues like most of us do, although as they get older they are often able to overcome some of the social issues they suffered from as a child.

If you want a successful relationship with an Aspie you need to understand how to communicate with them properly. You need to understand the syndrome at its very core. It can be hard to deal with someone who has Asperger's if you don't understand the reasoning behind their words and actions.

Throughout this book you will discover more effective ways to communicate with someone who has Asperger's. Not only will you understand more about the syndrome but you will also learn that great communication can come naturally using the right techniques.

Thanks again for downloading this book. I hope it serves you well on your journey to greater understanding of the ins and outs of Asperger's.

Chapter 1: Dr. Asperger and the Little Professors

A patient went to her doctor and was referred to a consultant. He told her that her symptoms might show she had a rare syndrome. If she had this syndrome it would mean she should be prepared for some pretty horrible developments, and there was no cure. He offered her a simple diagnostic test – or she could just go away and hope for the best.

The patient hesitated. She imagined going home and wondering every day whether she had the syndrome. "It's better to know," she decided.

This is a true story, although the consultant wasn't talking about Asperger's. In fact the test came back negative. The patient didn't have a rare syndrome, but neither did she have an explanation for her symptoms.

Chances are that you're reading this book because you suspect, or have been told, that someone you love has Asperger's

Syndrome. It may even be you. Maybe it's been a bit of a shock. You may even be in denial. You're probably wondering how you're going to cope.

Some people, on the other hand, may be looking for answers to explain some pretty puzzling instincts in themselves or odd behavior patterns in a loved one. For them, a positive diagnosis would provide an explanation for something that's been troubling them, possibly for years. In this case a verdict of Asperger's Syndrome would come as a welcome relief.

Whatever your reasons for reading, it's better to know. "Knowledge is power," and understanding Asperger's will give you the power you need to recognize and cope with your loved one's behavior.

Let's start at the beginning, and cut a big diagnosis down to bite-size portions by taking a look at the name.

What's all this about a Syndrome?

Firstly, why is it called a syndrome? In fact, even the term "syndrome" can be confusing. Is a syndrome the same as a disease? If so, why complicate things by having both terms?

The answer is no, a syndrome is different from a disease. A disease is a health condition where there is a clear underlying cause. The doctor can recognize the disease because the symptoms, or signs that something is wrong, are fairly obvious. They are also consistent; that is, all patients with the disease will show the same symptoms. The disease causes various changes in the body which can be picked up through blood tests, scans and x-rays, and so on. It is usually pretty straightforward to diagnose a disease and prescribe a suitable treatment if one is available.

A syndrome is different. It doesn't have any of these characteristics. The word "syndrome" is taken from the Greek for "run together," and this is a good description of the nature of a syndrome. It's more of a collection of symptoms taken together as a whole. These can include behavioral and emotional issues as well as physical symptoms.

This group of symptoms isn't consistent. It can vary from patient to patient. What's more, although there may sometimes be changes in the body's structure, or anatomy, the symptoms can't be traced back to a single cause. Take Chronic Fatigue Syndrome, for example. The main symptom, not surprisingly, is fatigue, or tiredness, which can be caused by plenty of other things. No wonder it can take doctors a long time to diagnose it.

A syndrome does not have any cure as such because it has no obvious single cause. However, doctors may be able to prescribe medication, or any other forms of treatment that may be available, to help relieve the different symptoms. Many people living with a syndrome just learn to find the best way to manage the condition, or help their loved ones manage it, by arranging their lifestyle around the symptoms and learning to watch out for the kind of situations that make them worse.

We don't know the reasons why syndromes occur, although sometimes they run in families. It's all rather vague in comparison to a disease. In fact, syndromes are one of nature's medical mysteries.

Dr. Hans Asperger

What about the first part of the name? Asperger's Syndrome is named after an Austrian psychiatrist and pediatrician, Dr. Hans Asperger (1906-1980). He produced a paper on autism in 1944, which was based on his studies of a small number of high-functioning autistic children.

His work is considered a little controversial and in fact it has been dismissed by some experts. This is partly because Dr. Asperger's work was published in German during World War II and wasn't translated into English until 1991, some 11 years after his death and half a century after his original studies were carried out.

One of the most interesting facts about Hans Asperger is that, ironically, he seems to have had some characteristics we might typically associate with Asperger's. As a child he was a loner who had difficulty making friends. He was intelligent and loved memorizing poetry, which he would quote to the other children at school at some length, and often spoke about himself in the third person – "Hans likes poetry," and so on. Perhaps this is why he was drawn to study children with similar characteristics.

Dr. Asperger was a passionate supporter of these youngsters and called them his "little professors" because of their intelligence, their formal way of speaking and their habit of lecturing others about their interests. He named this condition "autistic psychopathy." But his study took place at a time when the ruling Nazi party, under Hitler, had a policy of eugenics – that is, eliminating those they classed as unfit in an attempt to create a master race. Anyone who was considered mentally deficient was in danger of sterilization or even death.

Dr. Asperger believed high-functioning autistic children could become extraordinary achievers as adults because of their love of detail and ability to memorize facts and figures. However, he realized that the Nazis wouldn't appreciate that point of view and "his" boys could be at risk.

In his paper Asperger passionately defends them from being categorized as mentally deficient. "We are convinced, then, that autistic people have their place in the organism of the social community," he wrote. "They fulfill their role well, perhaps better than anyone else could, and we are talking of people who as children had the greatest difficulties and caused untold worries to their caregivers." (*'Autistic psychopathy' in childhood*, 1944.)

So if Asperger didn't name the syndrome, where does the name "Asperger's Syndrome" come from? It was first coined by a British psychiatrist, Dr. Lorna Wing, in 1981. She had an autistic daughter herself and had founded the National Autistic Society as far back as 1962. She chose the name

"Asperger's Syndrome" because it was a neutral-sounding term which avoided using the word "psychopathy" and its modern association with sociopathic behavior.

Asperger's Syndrome became a separately recognized condition in 1992, although its links with autism were still very strong. Some medical experts believe that Asperger's can't be distinguished from high-functioning autism, and in fact they are now both classed under the umbrella term "autistic spectrum disorders." We'll be looking at this in the next chapter.

So what is Asperger's Syndrome?

Asperger's Syndrome is a developmental disorder. We could describe it as a collection of symptoms which mainly have to do with mental processes and behavior. As it's on the autistic spectrum, or range of conditions, Asperger's is closely related to autism; in fact, as we've just seen, it's generally viewed as a kind of autism.

However, there are some big differences between Asperger's and the rest of the autistic spectrum. Children with Asperger's Syndrome lack social skills and find it difficult to make friends, but on the whole they have a more normal learning development and are able to learn better communication skills than a child with more severe forms of autism.

Looking forward

There are no physical signs or distinguishing features with Asperger's, unlike there are with other developmental disorders such as Down's syndrome, for example. Apart from any behavioral or social problems which may suggest that something isn't quite right, it's impossible for a stranger to tell by looking at someone whether or not they have Asperger's. This means that a child with Asperger's Syndrome who learns to manage the condition as he or she grows up will be able to live a near-normal life and function very well in society.

People with Asperger's may be limited by repetitive patterns of thought or behavior, but they are often highly intelligent. They can learn to cope with the disorder – for example, by establishing and maintaining routines – and may use their absorption with minute details to create an eminent career. A great many people with Asperger's are able to mask their problems; some may not be diagnosed until they are adults, and possibly not even then. For this reason it's impossible to estimate the total number of people with Asperger's Syndrome alive today.

There have been thousands of studies, many of which are ongoing. It's very likely that one day in the not too distant future we will understand far more about the condition, what causes it and possibly even how it can be prevented.

Chapter 2: The Autistic Spectrum

Asperger's Syndrome is classed as an autistic spectrum disorder. What does that mean?

Before we talk any more about Asperger's, let's take a look at the autistic spectrum and why it's important.

The word "spectrum" here means a range of conditions. Not all people with autism have the same problems. So the autistic spectrum really translates as "a range of conditions associated with autism." But this range is pretty wide and covers a whole array of symptoms and problems.

Some children on the spectrum will have a devastating level of disability and will need to be cared for in an institution; others will have a milder handicap and be able to live a more or less normal life with a few significant limitations. This last category is what is meant by "high-functioning autism."

The symptoms vary so much that now a single category is used to describe this kind of developmental syndrome: autistic spectrum disorder.

Autism – a different planet?

Autism is a complex developmental disorder, known as a "pervasive development disorder" (PDD). Or, to put it more simply, it's a brain disorder that affects a child's development. Sometimes it may be evident soon after birth, but it normally becomes obvious that something's not right when the child starts school or even preschool and begins interacting with other children. Sometimes it may not be spotted right away, or it may be dismissed as just a slight delay in some areas of development.

Autism mainly affects behavior, language skills and social interaction. A child or adult with an autistic spectrum disorder can range from someone who can't communicate at all to someone who just has trouble understanding other people's feelings.

A child with autism may have clumsy, rigid movements, repetitive behaviors, and of course trouble communicating with others. This isn't just because of their poor language development but because they don't have a major skill most of us pick up as little children: they can't "read" faces, body language or social signs. They can't tell what someone else is thinking or imagine how someone is feeling, and this puts them at a big disadvantage in any situation involving another person or group of people.

If you think about it for a minute, you can see how this inability to pick up on other people's emotions must make life extremely difficult for someone with autism. Not only do they miss out on the signs we all recognize when talking to others, but they can't fully express themselves either, not just in words but through their facial expressions and body language.

Reading the signs

All of us rely on what is known as "nonverbal communication" in our interactions with other people. We watch their eyes, their body language and especially their expressions, and tend to mirror what we see in our own faces and body language. So what happens when you can't see, or you can't make sense of what you see?

When someone loses their sight they lose a whole load of instinctive communication with it, because just hearing someone's voice doesn't tell the whole story. How is this person feeling? What are they thinking? What do they think about *me* – are they giving me their full attention and looking me in the eye, for example, or do they keep looking at their watch? Are they looking around for someone else to talk to?

50 shades of communication

Someone who loses their sight will eventually become sensitive to other people's voices. Their hearing will begin to compensate and supply some of the answers. But someone with autism will never fully understand all the complex shades of social interaction.

At best an autistic spectrum child may learn what's expected of him, and how to relate to those about him, but it never becomes instinctive. Even a high-functioning adult will sometimes use inappropriate language, conversation or behavior.

Just think of the whole complicated area of relationships and the different ways we behave with different people: a family member, a stranger, a co-worker or an employer, for example. We know the acceptable ways to talk to each one and the things that are best left unsaid. No one would tell their boss about a great night out on the town, for example, and how much they had to drink; but it would generally be fine to tell a colleague. Likewise you wouldn't share with a stranger the kind of intimate conversation you might have with a girlfriend.

Now imagine trying to explain these unwritten rules to someone from a different planet – not to mention the issues of small talk, humor, tactfulness, banter, irony and respecting confidentiality. The whole area of social chitchat which we take for granted is a minefield for the innocent.

Hypersensitivity and other challenges

Many people on the autistic spectrum experience other issues too, and the communication problems make everything more difficult as the autistic child can't tell us how he feels and why he behaves in this way.

For example, some children seem to be hypersensitive and become very anxious around certain everyday things – a sound, a smell, a sight or even a touch – which may not just distress them but actually appear to cause them pain. This is completely bewildering to most parents or caregivers because we can't identify with it. At best we can learn to accept it as a given for our loved one and find a way to work round it.

Let's look at an example of this hypersensitivity. An 11-year-old boy had been introduced to baking and it became one of his major interests. But along with the pleasure he found in baking came extreme pain, which seemed to be caused by the touch of the dough on his hands.

Instead of giving up, he was encouraged to persevere wearing plastic gloves so his skin didn't come into contact with the mixture, and in this way he was able to continue to enjoy his new hobby. What he really loved too was plunging his hands, still wearing the gloves, into soothing water after the session.

It is quite common for an autistic child to have repetitive behaviors or body movements, such as rocking or hand wringing. They need to have settled routines and will become resistant, even aggressive, to any changes in this routine. This aggression may be directed towards their parent or caregiver, or against themselves. And at other times they seem to withdraw from their surroundings and be unaware of the people around them.

Children on the autistic spectrum will develop better in some skills than others. Not every area of development is delayed, and in some areas they may show an amazing amount of talent. This may be in a creative field, such as drawing or playing a musical instrument; or it may be in more intellectual areas like math, learning poems or memorizing lists of facts. Autistic spectrum children may rank above average on nonverbal intelligence tests.

Asperger's and the autistic spectrum: where does it fit in?

Asperger's Syndrome is usually thought of as a mild form of autism. That means that on the range of developmental disorders which make up the autistic spectrum someone with

Asperger's is high-functioning and stands a good chance of living a relatively normal life.

Having said that, nothing is straightforward! Even within a diagnosis of Asperger's Syndrome there is a lot of variety from person to person. Not everyone with Asperger's has all the symptoms, and some may be affected more severely while others only have a mild disability which they can learn to conceal.

Some people with Asperger's even slip through the net because their symptoms have never been spotted and are not diagnosed until later in life, if at all. We all know people who are maybe a little eccentric: awkward conversationalists, people who blurt out inappropriate comments or who are obsessed with facts and figures about their area of expertise. They may not necessarily have Asperger's, but it goes to show how easy it can be to miss being diagnosed.

Asperger's vs. high-functioning autism: head to head

As we have seen, there are such strong similarities between Asperger's Syndrome and high-functioning autism that the lines can become blurred. In fact, some experts feel that these two conditions on the autistic spectrum are actually one and the same, and that they shouldn't even be classed as autism at all. This is mainly because a key indication the two conditions have in common is average or even above-average intelligence.

So is Asperger's Syndrome the same as high-functioning autism, then? The answer is yes and no, because although they have similarities, there are also differences. In fact, there is a significant difference in development between young children with Asperger's and those with high-functioning autism, and it has to do with how they learn to talk.

With Asperger's Syndrome there is usually little delay at first in language development; the child learns to speak and picks up a few words at about the same rate as any other toddler. Then after a while it becomes obvious that they don't seem to

23

be learning any more words, despite encouragement from their parents. So although there is a delay in language development it comes along later. Those with any kind of autism, on the other hand, including high-functioning autism, have much slower language development in the first place.

Despite this significant difference, children with Asperger's do have symptoms in common with the rest of the autistic spectrum, and these similarities seem to confirm that Asperger's Syndrome is a kind of mild autism.

These similarities include being clumsy, having poor social skills, and not understanding language when it's used in an abstract way (for example, idioms and humor), as these children take it literally. As we've already seen, they tend to have an obsession with facts and figures or particular items, and strong reactions to a range of textures, sounds, smells and so on which other people barely notice. We've already mentioned most of these areas in connection with autism, and they're often significant too for people with Asperger's Syndrome.

But there's another significant, and rather tragic, difference that separates people with Asperger's and high-functioning autism from those with other autistic spectrum disorders.

Importance of integration

Unlike those who are more seriously affected, people with Asperger's Syndrome and high-functioning autism are able to understand the world around them, and generally they want to be part of it. They want to get involved, but they don't know how to join in. They make mistakes because they can't read other people, and this can lead to teasing, bullying, anxiety, depression and social isolation.

So the greatest service parents and caregivers can do for these children is to learn how they can help them understand our world and fit in.

What if your loved one is already an adult? Well, there are still ways you can help them adjust and belong, and we'll be looking at this in a later chapter.

Chapter 3: Could it be Asperger's?

In this chapter we're going to take a look at the signs that may suggest that someone has Asperger's Syndrome.

Of course, many people reading this book will be looking for answers about their child's development or behavior, so some of these signs apply more to children. However, for some people the diagnosis may come much later. If you are wondering about your adult friend or your spouse, these signs still apply to some degree, although the adult may have learned to adjust or conceal them to some extent.

Unlocking potential

No parent wants to know that their child isn't "normal." Everyone's idea of growing up and having a family of their own assumes that the picture will include a certain number of cute, intelligent and good-looking kids. They'll be well adjusted with plenty of suitable friends, grow up to show concern for others less fortunate than themselves, have a good career, find a great partner and make their fond parents proud by earning enough money to support them in their old age. Right?

Well, you may be surprised to learn that even if your child does have Asperger's Syndrome, he or she may well meet many of those targets.

People with Asperger's can be cute, intelligent and good-looking; remember, you can't tell by appearances that someone may have Asperger's. Because of their above-average intelligence they can be high achievers and have a great career, thanks to their creative abilities and fascination with their fields of interest. And they have a good chance of finding a loving partner and having a long, happy marriage with someone who understands them. What parent wouldn't be proud?

So don't despair. You have a great kid, partner or friend with a lot of potential.

However, it's not going to be a walk in the park. Your loved one has potential, but it needs to be unlocked. So although he or she may meet many of those targets we just mentioned, they'll need a bit of help to get there. And some of the other ambitions, like being a well-adjusted member of society, might be even more challenging. As we saw in the last chapter, an "Aspie" doesn't see the world as we see it, so they're going to need help if they're ever going to fit in.

Parents, siblings, caregivers and teachers are the biggest keys when it comes to unlocking a child's potential. They are around every day and will play a greater role in a child's life than anyone else at this stage. Of course, as people get older this role tends to be taken over by other influential adults, such as their spouse or partner, co-workers and friends.

Putting the signs together

It may be that you already have a diagnosis, or that your loved one is now going through a series of tests. But sometimes parents who are wondering about their child put off the fateful moment when they have to make an appointment to raise the issue with their doctor. Either they haven't noticed anything wrong, or they put it down to a minor delay in development. Or sometimes they're just plain scared.

When it comes to wondering about a spouse, partner or friend who may have Asperger's, the situation becomes more complicated. When should you mention your thoughts to them? Suppose your loved one has no idea his behavior is a little off – what would that do to their confidence? How would they feel about not being diagnosed and starting therapy earlier?

Most times parents pick up on the fact that something may be wrong once their toddler is old enough to go to preschool and mix with other little ones. In fact, it may be the staff at the preschool who first spot the signs. But as this is an unsettling time for children the fact that there may be problems interacting with others isn't a clear sign on its own that something's amiss.

No two Asperger's cases are exactly the same, but here are some of the areas you should be looking out for. Bear in mind, though, that if you notice something from this list it doesn't necessarily mean the person has Asperger's Syndrome, or is on the autistic spectrum at all; it's just a pointer for you to monitor. Your loved one would need to have a combination of several symptoms to be diagnosed with Asperger's, so here are the things the doctor will be looking out for.

Social interaction

As we saw in the last chapter, the key problem for someone with Asperger's lies in their inability to interact with others. If your loved one seems to be having significant problems in social settings it could be a big sign of a possible autistic spectrum disorder. So watch out for situations where he or she fails to interact in a normal way with others, like taking turns to speak and answer, begin a conversation or respond to another person. This is not the same as a shy, nervous child who may be withdrawn but will still acknowledge other people.

One example of this trait is two boys who were both fascinated by the same computer game and spent hours playing it. However, instead of a friendship forming naturally based on this shared interest, the boys misinterpreted the situation and viewed it as a competition. They became rivals instead of friends.

Routines

People with Asperger's Syndrome like their routines. You may not notice the routine – for example, always getting dressed in the same order – but you'll notice what happens when the routine is changed!

Of course, having a routine is no big deal; in fact, a lot of children (and adults) like to stick to the same pattern of doing things. It's a way of being organized which can make for great timekeeping and help with memory skills. On the other hand, life isn't particularly organized and we have to be fairly flexible to cope with things outside our control. People with Asperger's Syndrome have problems with flexibility.

Empathy

You may have noticed that your child, friend or partner never seems to show sympathy or kindness to others. Of course, children have to be taught and frequently reminded to "be nice," but someone with Asperger's, like others on the autistic spectrum, usually doesn't respond to someone crying or in pain, or experiencing other strong emotions.

An adult "Aspie" won't pick up on the signals that you've had a bad day, or you're having problems at home or at work. It seems they can't empathize with others because they don't read the signs and know how someone feels. Even if you tell them, they may well not realize you could do with a little support or a chance to let off steam unless you spell out what you need from them.

Language

People with Asperger's Syndrome are pretty literal. They may not get jokes, metaphors and idioms, for example. One worker at a charitable organization helping children with Asperger's needed to get some advice. She turned to another worker and asked if she could "pick her brains." A child nearby overheard and started screaming!

Experts believe people with Asperger's find it hard to pick up on the different tones and pitches we use in everyday language to change the meaning of the words we say. In fact, their speech can be flat too, without normal inflexions and tones. This can make them a little difficult to understand.

But despite the lack of inflexion their speech can be pretty advanced in other areas, and in fact a young child might speak in a grown-up, formal way which can actually be quite endearing. They might use longer words or more complex words than other children; a simple example might be saying "return" instead of "come back." However, children do tend to pick up some of their parents' phrases and mannerisms, so again on its own it's probably nothing to worry about.

Obsessions

People with Asperger's like to talk, especially about their favorite subjects. They don't understand about holding a conversation so there is little interaction with anyone else. It's all a bit one-sided, and may include speaking their thoughts out loud.

Both children and adults with Asperger's Syndrome tend to have a very small field of interest and can be preoccupied, even obsessed, with their favorite subject. They know everything about this subject and collect facts and details about it.

Children can be fascinated by unusual interests, focusing on one area over and above anything else, and can become very knowledgeable. (You may remember Hans Asperger called them his "little professors" because of this trait and their formal way of speaking.) Their handwriting may be poor, but they can be capable of intricate drawings and pictures.

Physical symptoms

Although to the casual observer people with Asperger's Syndrome don't look any different from others, they may have a strange way of standing, sitting and so on, or use odd facial expressions. They might stare at other people or avoid eye contact altogether. Asperger's children might walk a little awkwardly and take longer than other kids to learn physical tasks, like handling cutlery or catching a ball, because of a delay in motor development —that is, movement and coordination.

And as we saw in the last chapter, people on the autistic spectrum seem to be highly sensitive to different sounds, textures, lights and tastes. One 10-year-old would only eat toast or plain pasta due to extreme taste sensitivity. A 14-year-old girl couldn't bear to hear someone whispering because it was painful. And it's quite common for them to have all the labels removed from their clothes, and even to only wear duplicates of the same outfit because nothing else is comfortable.

Many "normal" people have one or two of the traits on this list. A doctor isn't going to decide someone has a problem just because he fits the bill in a couple of areas. However, if your loved one has some of these characteristics and *also* has problems interacting with others in the way we described earlier, he or she may be on the autistic spectrum.

If you're the parent, you should make that appointment; if you're a friend, partner or spouse, it could be time to have that conversation.

Chapter 4: Assessment and After

Let's assume that you've noticed a few of the signs we mentioned in the last chapter and you're beginning to think your loved one (most often a child) may have Asperger's Syndrome. Maybe someone else has noticed something; a teacher may have suggested your child should be assessed for an autistic spectrum disorder, for example, because of the behavior patterns they've observed in school or preschool.

It's a scary thought and one you'd rather not have to face. But putting off the moment when you get a proper diagnosis isn't going to help anyone.

Do we need an assessment?

Even if you remain in denial, more people are going to start noticing if something really is amiss. So let's face it: it's time to make that appointment with the doctor and start the ball rolling. Remember the patient right at the beginning of this book who faced a difficult diagnosis? It's better to know, because the sooner you have a diagnosis the sooner you can start getting your child the help he needs.

If you are concerned about an adult who may have missed being diagnosed with Asperger's Syndrome as a child, the situation is different. Although you can offer advice and support the final decision rests with them, not you.

Some people may be aware that they see the world differently, but they don't want to be diagnosed or "labeled." They may have adapted quite well to the world around them and, even though life could maybe be better with a diagnosis and therapy, they might be unwilling to be assessed.

On the other hand, for many people a diagnosis of Asperger's Syndrome is a lightbulb moment, a turning point in their lives when they realize for the first time why their social and communication difficulties are preventing them from fitting into society.

40

Even though you may not be able to arrange an assessment for your partner or friend, you still have a role to play in everyday encouragement and support. In the next chapter we'll begin looking at practical hints and tips to help anyone living with an Asperger's sufferer learn how to help them.

Some parents or caregivers may feel they don't need to get a formal assessment for their child or teenager and can make an educated guess based on a list of symptoms. Please don't be tempted to do this; it's very important that anyone with a possible autistic spectrum disorder is seen by a professional and gets an accurate diagnosis to access specialist help.

It could be that you've already made the appointment and your loved one is scheduled for assessment. Now you're wondering what to expect. Do you know what the doctors will be looking for? Or maybe your child, friend or partner has already been assessed and you've been told he or she has Asperger's. How do doctors know for sure? And where do we go from here?

Testing for Asperger's Syndrome

What kinds of tests take place when a doctor needs to assess someone for Asperger's? Well, he or she will first find out whether they meet the basic criteria for Asperger's Syndrome. As we've already seen, these include problems interacting with others, showing unusual behavior, and being preoccupied with strange interests and activities. But the other criteria are that the patient did start speaking, crawling and walking at a normal age and shows an interest in the environment he lives in.

If your loved one meets these criteria, the doctor will probably want to have input from people who are part of your loved one's everyday life and, for an adult, people who were part of their early life. So for a child this might be parents and teachers, and maybe babysitters, grandparents, other medical professionals, and so on. For an adult, who may no longer have their parents or teachers to talk about their childhood, it might include siblings, close friends and work colleagues.

All this is so that the doctor can build an accurate picture of the patient's development and abilities. He may take a full medical history, which will probably look at the mother's pregnancy and the family's medical conditions, especially when someone else in the family has a developmental disorder. Asperger's Syndrome is thought to run in families to some extent.

Assessing abilities

The doctor will probably refer the patient to a specialist, who will carry out the tests used to confirm Asperger's. These involve various assessments to help build a full picture of what's going on, especially when the patient is a child.

First there will be a psychological assessment to test their intelligence, learning abilities and possibly their motor skills. Sometimes a personality assessment is carried out too.

What next? Well, there'll be a communication assessment to evaluate the patient's speech and language. This tests how much he or she understands and uses language to express ideas. The specialist also tests how much they understand nonverbal communication, such as reading another person's body language or facial expressions.

Then there may be an evaluation of their voice for tone and pitch, and how much they pick up on changes in tone and pitch in other people's voices. These are clues which help us identify when someone is using language in a nonliteral way, such as humor, sarcasm or metaphors.

There will probably be a psychiatric examination to assess how much the patient is able to understand other people's feelings, how they react to new situations and how they cope with indirect communication. This would include whether they can understand teasing or banter, for example. In some cases the specialist might also test for conditions like depression and anxiety, which people with Asperger's Syndrome often have due to their inability to understand and fit in with others.

To test for all this the specialist will probably observe your child both at home and at school to see how they interact in everyday settings with those around them. An adult may be observed in the workplace or in social environments.

A tailor-made program for your "Aspie"

If you've been told that your child, partner or friend has Asperger's Syndrome, don't panic! You're in the best possible position now to help him or her. The assessment will show the area or areas where your loved one will need most support. This is especially so for children, who are still developing and also can't express themselves as well as adults.

As we said right at the beginning, there is no cure for syndromes as such, but the doctor may prescribe medication to help with certain symptoms if necessary. For example, some of the behavioral problems associated with Asperger's Syndrome may be linked to other conditions, like attention-deficit hyperactivity disorder (ADHD), obsessive-compulsive disorder (OCD) and bipolar disorder. If your child or partner has symptoms associated with these conditions they can usually be helped with medication and other forms of therapy which your doctor can prescribe or recommend.

Now that your loved one has been diagnosed, he or she is in a position to receive professional support on an ongoing basis, so don't feel that you both have to face an uncertain future with no help from outside. There is much more awareness of autistic spectrum disorders now; in the US, as with many other countries, Asperger's is classed as a disability. There are plenty of support groups and sources of information out there, so you are not on your own.

Even though there's no cure as such, it's important not to imagine that nothing can be done to help someone with Asperger's Syndrome. There is treatment available to help an

Asperger's child understand the world around them and learn how to fit in. But parents will have to be proactive by working with schools, teachers, other caregivers and the medical professionals to work out what is best for their child.

Making the difference early on

A mother was lamenting the fact that her son had only just been diagnosed at age 11. She was concerned because he'd missed out on years of professional help. But the child psychiatrist pointed out how far they had come without even knowing what the matter was, and what a great job she had done on her own. His praise and encouragement gave her the strength to carry on, because her love and support were what had made all the difference to her child.

No two cases of Asperger's Syndrome are quite the same, because it varies so much from person to person. Some have problems that others don't have; some will be seriously affected in one area but not in others, and so on. This means that there isn't a "one size fits all" solution.

Instead, each treatment plan addresses the symptoms of an individual – especially children, who need the most help in order to benefit from school and learn social and communication skills to get on with others – and each individual's plan works to support them in the areas where they need the most help. So it has to be carefully tailored to each individual to meet their particular needs.

We've seen earlier in the book how the person with Asperger's usually wants to join in and mix with others, but fails because of their inability to understand and interact with other people. This can lead to teasing, bullying, anxiety, loneliness, and depression. So when we think about treatment for Asperger's sufferers, especially children, this is the scenario we are aiming to avoid. Everything is geared to helping them understand the world about them and learn to fit in.

Working with the school

In the US, federal law requires public schools (that is, state schools) to provide suitable facilities for teaching children and young people with disabilities right up to age 21. There may be more policies at a local or state level. So you should start by talking to your local school district and finding out what services are available in your area.

You then need to meet with staff at your child's school or preschool to talk about his needs and work with them to draw up a detailed plan which aims at offering support to meet those needs. This is called an Individualized Education Program, which is tailored to meet the specific requirements of your child based on the findings of the assessments.

You can take a look at the services on offer at various schools in your area and decide which one would be most helpful for your child. The best pointers to look out for include those offering plenty of individual attention in small groups, with opportunities to interact with others under supervision, and a flexible curriculum which can be tailored to give extra support where your child needs most help.

Other excellent features include an emphasis on encouraging each child's gifts and interests, an open attitude which embraces diversity among students, experienced staff with excellent communication skills, and the ability to provide training for children in social awareness and the practical tasks of daily life.

Consistency is key

In addition to these very valuable services, you should remember that communication is a vital part of supporting your child through the stresses and strains of school life. Ideally you should have someone to liaise with at the school – either a teacher or a counselor – who will give you feedback on your child's progress and wellbeing.

A communication diary is a great idea for day to day reports; it can go back and forth from home to school to make sure the teacher is aware of any new developments at home, and vice versa. It will also help to maintain consistency, which is vital.

The increased awareness about Asperger's, which has resulted in more facilities and training in schools, has also led to a rise in the number of charitable organizations run by dedicated, experienced volunteers in many areas. They are a great source of support and encouragement for both your child and the rest of your family.

Don't lose sight of the goal

Remember, the long-term objective for anyone with Asperger's is for them to be able to live independently in the community once they have reached adulthood. This means that everything both you and the school do for your child on a daily basis is aimed towards meeting this end, helping them learn how to interact with others and blend in, as comfortably as possible, as a fully functioning member of society.

If your "Aspie" is an adult, chances are he or she has found ways to adapt to the world around them, even though they may not completely understand why they find it hard to fit in. The aim is still to help them interact and communicate with others, be able to enjoy social relationships, avoid isolation and make the most of their particular gifts and interests.

Chapter 5: Coping Strategies

In this chapter we're going to be looking at ways of managing the situation that apply equally well to adults, children and teenagers.

As you will have noticed, when someone you love has Asperger's Syndrome life can get very challenging at times for the rest of the family! The need for a regular routine, misunderstandings over language and emotional situations, and a focus on limited areas of interest can all affect relationships with loved ones.

In addition, the communication difficulties that someone with Asperger's experiences mean that it can be hard to come alongside them and offer the help they need. Some may suffer from behavioral issues, aggression, mood swings and concentration problems too, making it even harder to offer support when it's needed.

Although awareness is increasing, other people may have difficulty understanding what's happening. A child with Asperger's Syndrome has poor social skills which may mean fewer invitations to birthday parties and sleepovers, for example. Adults with Asperger's may come over as rude, over-intense or bored. It can all make life pretty lonely for both the patient and for you.

Strategic steps for supporting your "Aspie"

Once your loved one has been diagnosed with Asperger's, there are things you can start to do straightaway. We're not talking about treatment plans now, or working with a child's school, although as we have seen they are vital too and should be continued to maintain consistency. Instead, these are steps you can take for yourself within the home, whatever the age of your loved one, so that you can learn to provide the support he or she needs.

Remember, you will almost certainly need other people to support *you* – friends, teachers, grandparents, employers, counselors – to offer encouragement and understanding, a shoulder to cry on, practical advice, or a chance to have a break. In particular you must make sure they understand the problems your loved one is facing. Once others understand, you no longer have to bear the burden alone, so help them to help you.

Having said that, there's plenty you can do by yourself. To start with, let's look at the first basic strategies you should introduce, if you haven't already done so.

Get organized

First, aim to establish routines. Make life as structured as possible. Routines are good, so stick to a regular schedule for everything as much as you can. Some Asperger's people like to have a timetable they can look at to keep everything clear in their mind - maybe a weekly and/or monthly chart on the wall with regular times and dates for appointments, shopping trips, social events, and so on.

Don't introduce changes unexpectedly. Of course there'll be times when a routine needs to change, but you should prepare your loved one as much as possible, starting well in advance and presenting the change in a positive way. Then introduce the change gradually so that it becomes easier for them to deal with.

Do your research

Second, find out all you can about Asperger's Syndrome, because understanding is a great key to being able to move forward. Not everything you read or hear will apply to you and your situation, but the more you know about the subject the more familiar it will become. You'll get some idea of how the world appears to someone with Asperger's and how you can help them, along with learning about treatment, therapies and specialists.

There's a great deal of information available online, and as well as helping you become an expert in your new specialism it will show you that there is plenty of support for other Asperger's families going through the same process.

Keep a diary

Third, you should also work towards understanding the particular issues facing your loved one and how he or she is affected by Asperger's. No two people are affected in quite the same way. Keep a diary or journal and note down the situations and environments that seem to be especially challenging for your child or partner. Look for patterns in their behavior and write down the solutions you try, the things to avoid, and the coping mechanisms you learn.

Many parents or partners come to realize, after a disastrous social event for example, that they had failed to prepare their loved one in advance, often because it never occurred to them. Things that we take for granted, like having friends round, need careful explanations beforehand. Who's coming, and why? What will we do? How should we behave while they're here? Keeping a journal can help you see these missed opportunities, analyze what went wrong and prepare more carefully next time.

Explain their limitations (within reason)

Fourth, make sure other people realize what your child can and can't do. Your child does not appear disabled, so you'll have to tell people who come into contact with him on a regular basis – siblings, grandparents, teachers, counselors, and so on – and what that means in practical terms.

For example, you should explain that just because he doesn't look at them it doesn't mean he isn't listening; or that he may have trouble joining in with group activities. Tell them too about any particular triggers you know so that they can avoid a situation which will upset your child.

If your loved one is an adult, you will obviously have to respect their right to confidentiality and not tell everyone about his or her Asperger's. Your spouse or partner is able to tell them himself if he wishes. The same applies to teenagers who are beginning to find their way in the world, especially those who are coping reasonably well. No teenager wants to be humiliated in front of their friends by well-meaning parents, so be careful who you tell.

Instead you could just share the information with a few of your closest friends who you see most often; you can then turn to them for support, invite them round or accept invitations from them, knowing that they will understand any social problems.

Create a backing team

Fifth, build a support team – family and friends, a babysitter who understands your child, medical professionals you can trust to help you with decisions about treatment. Look online or ask your doctor about Asperger's charities, help groups and other sources of support. A lot of these groups are run by very experienced volunteers who are able and willing to offer you advice. Build a team of supporters, and both your loved one and the rest of your family will feel the benefit.

There may be times when you feel at breaking point; it's quite understandable and nothing to be ashamed about. Don't try to keep stress bottled in, because eventually feelings have a way of bursting out and causing untold damage. You need to be able to share with someone on a regular basis.

You also need people to turn to in a crisis, for support, a shoulder to cry on or a chance to vent. Maybe a friend or family member can sit with your loved one while you have a few hours to yourself, or a local Asperger's group may be able to provide a sympathetic ear, even arrange a short break.

If your partner has Asperger's, he or she will have difficulty understanding your feelings. If you don't have friends close by, you should consider joining a local group or an online forum for Asperger's families, where you can share with others who know how you feel.

Building blocks and coping stones

These five points are the essential building blocks you need to use to begin creating your own coping strategy. Start putting them together and they will help you learn to cope successfully with some of the problems associated with Asperger's Syndrome, and in turn you'll be able to help your loved one.

In fact, to borrow a bricklaying analogy, a coping stone is the final stone on the top of a wall; by the time you've built your wall of building blocks and mortared them together with a load of experience, you'll find that your "coping" is pretty much in place.

So now we've looked at some of the basic strategies to put in place, what else could you be doing? Here are some practical suggestions to add to your building blocks.

Chapter 6: Practical Strategies to Make a Difference

So far we've looked at the signs and symptoms of Asperger's Syndrome, getting an assessment for your loved one, and learning how to help them, and yourself, through basic coping mechanisms.

In this chapter we're going to take some of the major problem areas for someone with Asperger's and see what you can do to help. How should you approach these challenges? Let's look at each one and examine practical ways in which you can make a difference going forward.

Most of these are relevant whether your loved one is an adult, a teenager or a child, but some are aimed at helping parents with young children. That's because as someone with Asperger's gets older they are able to make more sense of the world and learn how to fit in better, so the problems are not quite so acute.

Obsessions: building a bridge

People with Asperger's tend to focus on a limited interest which can absorb all their attention for hours at a time. The subject can often be completely baffling to someone else. One expert cites examples of children spending countless hours watching YouTube videos on subjects such as elevators, hand dryers or vacuum cleaners, for example, and talking about them the rest of the time!

However hard it may be, try to take an interest in their obsession. It's a way of building bridges between you.

Some years ago a mother found a way of using her children's obsession to establish a bond with them. She had twin four-year-old boys who both had Asperger's Syndrome. They spent hours on end lying on the floor, just spinning the wheels on their toy cars. She was in despair as she was unable to engage their interest or interact with them in any way.

One day she got down on the floor, lay beside them, and started spinning the wheels too. To her amazement they turned, looked her in the eye and smiled! It was a breakthrough moment; the boys began to thrive academically and socially, and years later are now at university.

With older children and adults, you may consider setting a time limit with them when they can talk about their interest with you. Arrange it for a fixed time each day. Try to be proactive by asking questions and listening to what they have to say.

Setting a time limit like this can also work with hobbies which he or she may be using as coping mechanisms; they are important, but they may take your loved one out of the house for hours at a time. One woman did it the other way round, and asked her partner for 100 minutes a week when they could be together.

Watch your language!

As we've seen, someone with Asperger's tends to take things literally. If you can avoid saying "I'll be with you in a minute" or "Just a second," it will make things a little easier. Taking the time to explain you need to finish something first can save a lot of trouble later!

In the same way, when you have to arrange a rendezvous try not to give a very specific time to meet up; instead of saying "1 pm," say "Between 1 and 1.15," to allow for delays. Most of us wouldn't start worrying until someone was 20 or 30 minutes late, but someone with Asperger's Syndrome will start getting anxious after just a minute or two. Try to text or call to keep them informed if you are running late.

It's very difficult to avoid using idioms as we use them without thinking, but once your child is old enough to understand you can explain that sometimes we say things we don't actually mean. Someone with Asperger's Syndrome can be completely bemused about the other ways we use words too. Try to avoid irony or sarcasm, for example, especially with young children.

Older children and adults can learn to accept our use of everyday language, even if they don't understand it. Teaching them about jokes, teasing, sarcasm and the more complex areas of tactfulness and confidentiality can help them here. Use practical examples, say from the television or overhearing other people's conversations, to help them identify when someone is joking, being tactful, and so on.

Some "Aspies" learn to stop and think things through before blurting out inappropriate or unwelcome comments, but because the whole area of people's feelings is unknown territory to them they have difficulty imagining why they should or should not say something. Role play can be a great way to teach conversational skills, and works well for both children and adults.

Friendships

What about making friends? Try to encourage your loved one's social life. Help him or her to read the signs of friendship in others. If someone brings your child a toy, explain that it's because they want to play with him. Point out when his behavior is inappropriate and encourage friendships with other bright children. Asperger's children are smart and can become bored with less intelligent classmates.

Most people with Asperger's only want one close friend, not a group of friends. As they get older they can be hurt and bewildered that their close friend is developing other friendships, or has a romantic interest in someone and wants to be alone with their girl- or boyfriend.

They will need help to understand that the degree of closeness they enjoyed in the past is normally part of a mature relationship between two adults. He or she may not realize that it's not acceptable to spend a lot of time with someone else's partner, for example.

If you are friends with an "Aspie," it's important to help them learn the social skills they need to make a wider circle of friends. That way they can avoid over-dependence on one or two people and the hurt that inevitably follows. Try to include them in small group activities, for example, or introduce them to someone else with similar interests. If you feel you need more time to yourself, don't just drop them – maybe you can agree a limit on the number of hours you spend together each week.

Social skills

Help an adult learn to cope with social occasions by arranging carefully planned events in non-challenging situations, such as having friends round for dinner. Explain to your loved one what will happen and why, and what you expect them to do.

One woman was very upset because her husband didn't acknowledge their guests but continued to watch TV. She realized he didn't understand, and the next time she remembered to explain the situation in advance and tell him what he should do when the guests arrived.

Someone with Asperger's will probably continue to have problems interacting socially with other people, even as an adult. There are ways you can help with this. It may be better to write things down, as it can make it much easier for them to understand and remember.

For example, when it comes to conversation skills you could consider writing them a script. Someone with Asperger's tends to talk about themselves or their interest, fails to pay any attention to the other person, then walks off without saying goodbye. Your script should clearly show that he or she can speak to the other person only for a couple of minutes, then ask a question, which lets the other person speak. After listening they should make some polite comment like "Nice to talk with you; now I have to go" before they leave. Again, this is a situation where a little role play can be a great help too.

Unusual talents and interests

People with Asperger's Syndrome can have an amazing degree of talent. One 13-year-old boy playing on his scooter had an ability to rival that of professionals on skateboards.

If your loved one is a child or a teenager, try to find out their special gift and nurture it. It could be invaluable to him in the future, as many go on to have a career based on their ability in their field of interest. Their focus on detail and all-consuming passion make them experts in their area.

In the short term, your praise and the respect of others will be important in building confidence. People with Asperger's are used to hearing criticism. Remember to pay compliments, point out when he or she does something well, and tell them you love them.

Despite any special abilities, someone with Asperger's will probably struggle to learn new skills or ideas, especially involving abstract concepts. You can help by working with them. Explain in advance that they shouldn't expect to get it right first time, so that failure won't put them off trying again. It may help to use aids like photos, role playing and so on, and break the task down into stages, mastering each one before moving on to the next.

Meltdowns and outbursts

Is there a strategy to cope with meltdowns? Yes, there is.

Firstly, when your loved one gets upset through frustration or anxiety, try to use a softly-softly approach. You need to remain calm, because if you are stressed then they will be even more so. By responding quietly you are helping them feel secure and then they can regain control.

Secondly, try to see things from their point of view. Listen and believe them, even if it doesn't make sense to you. Show you respect their feelings and opinions, and take a moment to decide how you should respond.

If you are the parent or caregiver, you could also consider switching diets. Some research suggests that a gluten- and casein-free diet helps improve behavioral problems in children with Asperger's.

If you decide to give it a try, bear in mind that you must be consistent – and that includes at other people's homes, school and anywhere else your child has a meal. As they are often picky eaters and dislike change in any way, it could be very difficult to introduce a new diet; you will have to take it very slowly and offer rewards for every tiny milestone passed.

Showing affection

One aspect of living with someone who has Asperger's, which can be hurtful to their parents or partners, is in the area of showing affection. They will probably not realize when you've had a bad day or why you need some support, and you will have to explain how they can help. Be as clear and specific as possible about what you need and how it will make you feel.

One woman with Asperger's, a wife and mother, described how she factored in "time for hugs". It didn't come naturally to her as she didn't feel the need to show or receive affection in that way, but she had learned it was important to her husband and children so she made a point of remembering to include it in her schedule.

This story is a good example of how Asperger's patients can learn how to show affection to other people. They may not get it, but they can come to realize that these things are important for their friends and families. However, as it's not instinctive this behavior must be explained and taught, which will need time and patience.

Relationship difficulties

When it comes to adult relationships, the general ups and downs of domestic life are multiplied ten times over when one of the couple has Asperger's. It's important not to blame the other person for every fight or argument, because nine times out of ten you will both be at fault – for not fully understanding each other.

The writer Cindy Ariel suggests making a chart of three columns to try to work out what your partner may have been thinking in a particular situation. Why did he act like he did? Can you both learn from this instead of just having to put up with the situation?

In the first column, enter the situation that has annoyed or upset you; for example, "Didn't show any concern when I was sick in bed." In the second, outline how this made you feel – for example, "lonely and sad, as though he didn't care about me." In the third column, based on your understanding of Asperger's and experience of your partner, find an explanation

75

for their behavior. In this case it might be "Likes to be left alone when he's not feeling well."

It's very useful to think of the situation from the other's point of view. It's even more helpful if you both do it and then discuss the results.

Asperger's is a learning curve for everyone in the family, but it does get easier. Coping strategies like these, and many more to be found through support groups and online forums, will help you help your loved one – and yourself.

Chapter 7: Asperger's and the Workplace

Every parent has aspirations for their child's future. We want them to live a long and healthy life, marry a wonderful partner, live in a comfortable house in a great neighborhood and provide us with several beautiful grandchildren.

While most of us hope our kids will be happy too, we really want them to do as well as we did or even better. We want to be proud of them and be able to boast to our friends and neighbors about how much they have achieved.

To attain this happy-ever-after scenario we realize they need to do well at school and in due course work towards a secure future via a well-paid job or profession. But if you are a parent of a child or teenager with Asperger's Syndrome, your natural concerns about how well they do at school will be overlaid with anxiety about their future.

Making choices

So what does the future hold for Asperger's kids as they leave school? What kinds of jobs or careers are most suitable? And is it possible for an "Aspie" to be a high-flyer in their profession?

Well, it's fair to say that not every person with Asperger's will go on to have a successful career. Their social problems and communication difficulties can make it hard for them to shine at interviews, for a start. As we know, people with Asperger's Syndrome are highly intelligent, but that doesn't mean they do well in high-pressure situations. On the other hand, some people are able to cope well with pressure and stay cool when making difficult decisions.

The secret to success seems to be in their choice of career type.

People with Asperger's can excel in one of three kinds of positions, and knowing their strengths is vital when deciding what career path to follow. The first is the type of job that suits their need for routine and the security of a repetitive schedule, such as clerical or administrative work. These jobs are often dismissed as "boring" by others, so there is a relatively high turnover of staff. Employers are keen to find dedicated, focused individuals who are careful and conscientious about their work, and people with Asperger's can shine in these situations.

One woman found herself a job in a bookstore. It was ideally suited to her and she loved it: stocking shelves, arranging books in alphabetical order, memorizing lists of publishers, answering questions about particular books and authors. Her parents were slightly less pleased, because they felt with her high IQ she could have had a brilliant career. They felt she hadn't been able to fulfill her potential, but she was happy.

The second kind of career lies in using their intelligence, talent and preoccupation with detail to focus their skills on one small area of interest to businesses. Such experts can be highly sought-after, especially in technical or scientific industries.

It is said there are a high proportion of people with Asperger's in the Silicon Valley, because modern technology can be a great place for their skills. In fact, some employers are starting to look for people with Asperger's because, although they may not be team players, their intense focus and concentration, together with high IQs, make them excellent programmers, inventors and designers.

Going it alone

There is a third type of career choice for people with Asperger's Syndrome, although maybe not for everyone. They can be extremely successful entrepreneurs and business people.

Playing to their strengths, they are able to harness their focus, dedication and intimate knowledge of their own absorbing subject to become specialists in their field of interest. Their coolness under pressure and ability to make impersonal decisions can make them great leaders, and if motivating others or keeping them on board becomes a problem they can always hire someone to take on that role.

Working with an "Aspie"

If you are the manager or co-worker of someone with Asperger's (or who may have Asperger's), you will probably notice that while they are generally focused, diligent and careful workers they do struggle in certain areas. Let's take a look at these areas and what you can do to help.

Social interaction

This shows itself in inappropriate comments or behavior, being unable to understand what others are thinking or feeling, and misunderstanding or not "getting" nonverbal communication. As we've seen, these are all skills that someone with Asperger's does not know instinctively but has to be taught. Even if they were diagnosed as a child, an adult

"Aspie" may still struggle at times – even more so if they have never been diagnosed, although many have learned to conceal their problems.

In the workplace the best way to help avoid awkward situations is to give clear guidelines and establish rules, such as outlawing comments about anyone's physical appearance. Provide detailed instructions (in writing, if possible, or suggest they take notes and check verbally afterwards) about any task and what you expect them to do, so that they do not have to rely on nonverbal communication.

Mental processes

People with Asperger's can have problems with organization and time management. They may struggle to understand and carry through a task, especially if there's an element of multitasking involved, and by over-focusing they can miss deadlines. As well as providing detailed explanation and written guidelines, you may need to give further help – providing a mentor or offering flexible working hours are two possible solutions.

Sensory issues and stress

As we saw earlier, it is quite common for people with Asperger's Syndrome to have one or more sensory problems, such as intolerance of touch or sound. The modern workplace hums with electronic equipment, not to mention the sounds of people working or talking, phones ringing, and so on. And some people are affected, either visually or aurally, by the strip lighting which is common in offices and other workplaces.

Combined with the stress of coping with the people around them and the work they have been assigned, it's hardly surprising that at times someone with Asperger's Syndrome may go into sensory overload.

Many of these difficulties can be overcome by adjusting their working conditions. If possible offer a quiet workspace and alternative lighting. Giving the opportunity to get out of the work environment for a short break every hour or two, for example, can also be very helpful in relieving stress. You may even be able to arrange for them to work from home, either on a full-time or part-time basis.

The qualities of "Aspies"

Despite any difficulties, your employee or co-worker should be valued for the positive qualities they can bring to the workplace. As well as focused and conscientious workers, they are honest, loyal and dedicated, often taking great pride in their work and remaining with the same company for years. People with Asperger's are often great at making difficult decisions too, because they are not so influenced by emotions.

With a little help, someone with Asperger's Syndrome can be among your most valued staff members. It makes sense to accommodate their needs where possible, and these simple suggestions can make a great difference to their productivity.

Chapter 8: The Secret Life of an Aspie

So far we've looked at the basics of the autistic spectrum, the symptoms and assessment of Asperger's Syndrome, and some strategies for coping with and helping a loved one who has Asperger's.

In this chapter we'll be looking at Asperger's Syndrome from the point of view of people who have the disorder. What does it feel like? What does the future hold for someone growing up with Asperger's? And what is it like finding out you have Asperger's when you're middle-aged?

The columnist Matthew Rozsa, writing on the PolicyMic website on December 17, 2012, describes his struggle with Asperger's. "The defining characteristic of my childhood was my sense of being ineluctably 'different.' My interests were 'weird,' my personality was 'weird,' and not a day would pass without me discovering that I was completely wrong, either in my assessment of the impression my words and actions were making on others or the signals they were sending of what they thought and how they felt about me."

Blessing or curse?

It may come as a surprise after all we've learned about Asperger's, but many people with the disorder end up thinking of it as a kind of blessing. They may be proud of being different, their abilities and how far they've come.

Not everyone feels that way, of course; it's very difficult, especially as a child, to make any sense of a world which seems chaotic, noisy and confusing. That's where a caring, supportive family is so valuable. One young person with Asperger's says, "My mind was constantly whirring with thoughts, worries and concerns. The time spent with my obsession was the only time in which I had a clear mind - it gave me that much sought-after relaxation."

Others have compared having Asperger's to being in a different culture where you don't speak the language. A 15-year-old went further and described himself as an anthropologist, because he spent his life observing and trying to learn youth culture.

A sense of uniqueness

Older children and teenagers may start to accept their uniqueness and enjoy the sense of being out of the ordinary. As one 11-year-old boy put it, "I like being different. I like being unique. To be part of something that most people don't have makes me feel quite special."

Part of accepting themselves is learning to appreciate the exceptional aptitudes they have with Asperger's. An anonymous blogger on the site "Inside the mind of an Aspie" describes the awkwardness, stress and loneliness of feeling unable to cope in society, before going on to explain the positives.

"Asperger's gives me the ability to do things that most neurotypical people are not capable of. I'm able to think through most situations rationally, setting aside any emotions I may have and avoiding the biases that come with them. I'm able to process information faster than most people, which gives me the illusion of looking smarter – when in reality, my brain is simply more efficient at learning. I also have the ability to burden myself with painful situations and push through without falling apart mentally."

Inside knowledge

Thanks to the Internet, people are now able to express their feelings about having Asperger's and offer assistance and support to others. In fact, there are now sources online to help young people cope with school, employment and social situations. These have been written by people with Asperger's who have first-hand experience in working out how to cope; they can give plenty of practical suggestions in ways that people without the disorder can't, no matter how well-meaning or knowledgeable.

For example, one blog explains how to look someone in the eye without staring, how to have a conversation without talking too much, and how to decode their body language. These blogs and websites also make absorbing reading for parents, siblings and partners who wonder what life is like for their loved one.

Asperger pretense mode

Over the last few years, thanks to increasing awareness, widespread treatment programs and the Internet, there is more help available for people with Asperger's Syndrome than ever before. But despite all this, for many people life is a continuous pretense of being normal – sometimes called "Asperger pretense mode."

They describe the strain of constantly having to pretend to be someone they're not, concealing their real nature in order to be accepted and fit in with society's idea of "normal." Not surprisingly, sometimes they end up not knowing who they really are.

The fact that many still slip through the net and miss being diagnosed shows how effective this pretense can be. In fact, it's thought that this may be one explanation for why three or four times more boys than girls are diagnosed with Asperger's. Some experts suggest that girls are better at observing those around them and copying their behavior, so that their condition passes unnoticed.

Those people who slip through the net, both men and women, may spend years living so-called "normal" lives where nothing is really normal. They know they're not comfortable around other people and that they can't always make sense of things but don't really know why they don't fit in.

Sometimes they (or someone else) may wonder if they could have Asperger's Syndrome, but maybe they don't seem to fit all the criteria, especially as the textbooks are often geared towards diagnosing children. Some prefer not to know, and if taken to the doctor by a worried partner they continue with the pretense to avoid an assessment.

Making sense of it all

But most people are relieved to finally hear they have Asperger's Syndrome. The British singer Susan Boyle, who shot to worldwide fame after appearing on a TV talent show, recently made public the fact that she'd been diagnosed with Asperger's. Now in her fifties, Susan struggled for years with issues of confidence and anxiety, and experienced some well publicized episodes of volatile behavior when under pressure to perform.

Susan had been wrongly diagnosed as a child as having a mild form of brain injury from complications at birth. In an interview for the *Observer* newspaper on 8 December 2013, she said, "I was told I had brain damage. I always knew it was an unfair label. Now I have a clearer understanding of what's wrong and I feel relieved and a bit more relaxed about myself... It will not make any difference to my life. It's just a condition that I have to live with and work through."

Mark Ty-Wharton, on the website brookdalecare.co.uk, describes a breakthrough moment in his early 40s when he suddenly realized that his partner could instinctively read people's facial expressions. He was shocked to recognize it was something he could not do.

Mark started looking for answers, and when he was diagnosed all the other things he'd struggled with fell into place. "An Asperger's diagnosis helped me understand I am okay. It helps me communicate more effectively by taking autism into consideration and realizing I am actually comparatively normal. I have finally found a place where I fit."

Conclusion

Thank you for taking the time to educate yourself on Asperger's. You should now have a better understanding of what Asperger's is and how to deal with it—whether it is you or your loved one who is living with this syndrome.

If you take what you have learned in this book and apply it to your relationships you should see major improvements in your life. Whether your goal is for yourself or someone you know and love, I hope this book has empowered you to take action.

With the strategies you now have, you are definitely on the right path to more fulfilling ways of communicating in your life.

I wish you all the best and many years of prosperity and happiness.

Made in United States
Orlando, FL
18 December 2022

27240334R00059